Denny Dymes was born on September 25, 1962.

A high school graduate, Olney class of 1980, he wrote his first poem on mothers in 1994. Lately, he's been creating a sort of melody for some of his recent poems.

He likes to dabble in singing his poems and has created several YouTube videos.

My dad, Anthony P. Massei Jr. died when he was 55 years old. My mom, who is still with us and turns 83 on 20 February, encouraged me.

This book is sincerely dedicated to them.

Denny Dymes

FAITH AND INSPIRATION: VOLUME ONE

AUSTIN MACAULEY PUBLISHERS™
LONDON • CAMBRIDGE • NEW YORK • SHARJAH

Ordering Information
Quantity sales: Special discounts are available on quantity purchases by corporations, associations, and others. For details, contact the publisher at the address below.

Publisher's Cataloging-in-Publication data
Dymes, Denny
Faith and Inspiration: Volume One

ISBN 9798889102342 (Paperback)
ISBN 9798889102359 (ePub e-book)

Library of Congress Control Number: 2023922383

www.austinmacauley.com/us

First Published 2024
Austin Macauley Publishers LLC
40 Wall Street, 33rd Floor, Suite 3302
New York, NY 10005
USA

mail-usa@austinmacauley.com
+1 (646) 5125767

I'd like to thank everyone at Austin Macauley Publishers
for accepting my manuscript of poems and giving
me the chance to become a real published
author compared to self-publishing.

Table of Contents

1.
God Only Knows

Nights seem darker
storms are fiercer
people getting crazier each day
anymore, nobody likes to pray.
What ails the world?
God only knows
headed downward
steady as she goes.
The world is burning
a raging hell
but it keeps on turning
only God can make it well.
Calls for healing
will be answered
fall down to kneeling
it's time to pray.
What ails the world?
God only knows,
let's get together
and pray the world gets better.

2.

Jesus Come

My heart is all weary and sore
I don't want to live anymore,
Jesus come Jesus come
I am ready to go home.
My heart is feeling weary and blue
I know the Lord loves me true, Jesus come Jesus come
I am ready to go home.
I'm feeling depressed as of late
I have things on my mind that can't wait,
Jesus come Jesus come
I am ready to go home.
No, I don't want to live
I gave all I could give,
Jesus come Jesus come
I am ready to go home.
I've been through it all before
that's why my heart is sore,
Jesus come Jesus come
I am ready to go home.

10-27-2020

3.

Christmas Time is All for You

Every child's dreams
may them all come true,
to me it seems
Christmas Time is All for You.
Every little girl and boy
deserves all the joy,
your family loves you true
Christmas Time is All for You.
Your faces shine bright
in every Christmas light,
little angels precious and true
Christmas Time is All for You.
Santa Claus will soon be here
as your heart fills with cheer,
outside snow is falling right on cue
Christmas Time is All for You.

10-10-2020

4.
I Dreamed About Heaven Last Night

Through good times and bad
it's the best dream I ever had,
there was this light shining so bright
I dreamed about Heaven last night.
It is no mistake
I didn't want to awake,
from this dream I reveal
that seemed so real.
The pasture is so green
and trees, it's such a beautiful scene.
The sky, clouds and rain
this place where there's no pain,
if all goes right
I'd dream this dream every night,
this beauty I've never seen
so peaceful and serene,
by the grace of God, I'd stand by his holy light
if I can dream about Heaven every night.

10-15-2020

5.

I Don't Care If Tomorrow Never Comes

I don't have anything in this world to call my own
I am sad, broken hearted and alone.
Dear Lord if there's any love to share save me some
otherwise, I don't care if tomorrow never comes.
We are moving to a place where only good things I see
and I'm praying to the Lord if he will look after me,
many obstacles I see in our new home
and if God can't fix them then I don't care if tomorrow
never comes.
In this world of sorrow and woe
it's all I ever know,
if there's just a little peace save me some
or I won't care if tomorrow never comes.
If there's anything in this world I can cling to
it's all my memories I hold so true,
if there's any memories, you'd like to share send me some
otherwise, I don't care if tomorrow never comes.

09/20/2020

6.

I Repent My Sins

I repent my sins. Lord will you forgive me?
Come into my heart
so, my soul can be free.
I beg of you today
cleanse my soul, dear Lord, I pray.
Dear Lord, I open up my heart to you
I want to walk in your light,
tell me please what I should do
to make my darkened world so bright.
I'm searching for a better life
to escape my troubles and strife,
I know what I must do
repent my sins, dear Lord,
I need a friend like you.
I repent my sins, Lord will you forgive me?
Come into my heart
so, my soul can be free,
I beg of you today
cleanse my soul, dear Lord I pray.

07-12-2020

7.

Jesus on My Mind

I am thinking of Jesus as I do each day, he is on my mind too most of the night away.

Jesus so loving and so caring so kind, are the reasons I have Jesus on my mind.

I have the love of Jesus in my eyes, sometimes he cannot keep me happy

but I thank him when he tries.

Eternal peace he promised me after I am gone another great reason to believe and carry on.

Until the time comes from this life I depart; I will keep the love of Jesus in my heart. The love of Jesus flows all through me keeping my faith true to thee.

Every part of me deep within my soul it was my desire and lifelong goal, the love of Jesus for all to find in my heart and soul and forever on my mind.

By Dennis Andrew Massei
02-27-2020

8.

I Love to Tell the Truth

I love to tell the truth
in everything I do,
in everything I hear
Jesus is always near.
I love to tell the truth
in everything I see
the truth will make me free,
I love to tell the truth.
Lying is a mistake
all it proves that you're a fake,
it is my belief
lying's the cause of all your grief.
I love to tell the truth
I've done so my whole life through,
in my own humble way
the truth is all I can say.

By Dennis Andrew Massei
11-06-2020

9.

I Want Some Peace to Call Mine

If I can have just one thing
and if Jesus will bring,
I want to be
worry-free,
oh, where could I find
some peace of mind,
I want everything so fine
and I want peace to be mine.
No more troubles and strife
messing up my life,
if I could find
a little peace of mind,
it's all I require
to have everything I desire,
everything will be fine
if I had some peace to call mine.

By Dennis Andrew Massei
11-15-2020

10.
In the Back of My Mind

In the back of my mind
a poem you will find,
moving slowly toward the front
thinking hard hear me grunt,
pretty soon I will write
with all my rhyming might,
A poem about God peace and being kind,
or a poem about love, scenery, whatever's on my mind.
My thoughts basically
are what God taught me,
to help everyone who needs
love them and do good deeds.
bring peace, joy and cheer
do good throughout the year,
Simply being kind
these thoughts take center stage, in the back of my mind.

By Dennis Andrew Massei
12-08-2020

11.

Christmas Time Again

I can't wait till then

when it's Christmas time again a time for peace a time for rest people behaving their very best.

I remember way back when we were just little children acting the way we should girls and boys being good.

I look forward to this time of year when people act with grace and cheer spring, summer, winter and fall dear Lord grant my wish of good will to all.

Christmas time is worth the wait, hurry Santa don't be late I can't wait till then when it's Christmas time again.

By Dennis Andrew Massei
12-08-2020

12.

Not a Day Goes By

Not a day goes by
I don't think about my dad, though it's been years there are
times I still cry my dad my friend the best I ever had.
I'll love my dad my whole life through the day he died made
my heart weary and blue.
Christmas hasn't been the same since I lost my dad for if
someone calls his name it makes me feel sad.
I write this poem, it's all I can do to wish a Merry Christmas
to you.
Remembering the fun we had when I was a lad, not a day
goes by, Dad, I'll love you 'til the day I die.

By Dennis Andrew Massei
12-10-2020

13.

The Spirit of Christmas

The spirit of Christmas is here to fill our hearts with cheer and celebrate the day Christ was born when we wake up on Christmas morn.

Wrapping paper crinkling sound thrown all around as little children open their presents near the Christmas tree laughing and playing joyfully.

Spirit of Christmas everywhere, smell of chestnuts roasting fills the air children's faces says it all, smiling, giggling and having a ball.

The Spirit of Christmas is here soon we'll ring in a new year so have a Merry Christmas of white

I wish good will to all and to all a good night.

By Dennis Andrew Massei
12-11-2020

14.

If the Sky Falls Down

If the sky falls down all around

Jesus appeared and said let's go would you know somehow

that your life is over now?

Would you be ready to go right then?

Or ask a reprieve 'til when.

If the sky falls down all around

Jesus appeared

looked right at you what would you do?

Would you pray ask if you can stay for a little while or

would you smile say let's go

I'm ready now.

Would you accept and go with him and follow?

Will you decline and stay 'til you're forced away?

Will you know somehow that your life is over now?

By Dennis Andrew Massei
12-13-2020

15.
Make the Snow Go Away

Remember when snow was cool and there was no school
In the snow I'd play throughout the day.
Things aren't like they were before
I'm not a kid anymore
to God I pray
make the snow go away.
Now I have to shovel it
go to work, let's not forget
and run to the grocery store
things aren't like they were before.
Now I see snow in a different light
that messy pile of white
all I can say to God I pray
make the snow go away.

By Dennis Andrew Massei

12-16-2020

16.
Christmas

There's a big party going on up in Heaven
it's Jesus' birthday it doesn't get better than this
a day that's come to be known as Christmas
I can't wait 'til then.
The celebration is extended down here on Earth
the day of Jesus' birth
bring your friends and family together
to this party like no other
happy children with hearts filled with cheer
ready to welcome Santa here
that Christmassy smell fills the air
and the spirit of Christmas is everywhere.

By Dennis Andrew Massei
12-20-2020

MERRY CHRISTMAS FROM OUR HOME TO YOURS
AND MAY GOD BLESS US WITH MANY MORE.

17.

Color Me Blue

When I'm feeling low down
just color me blue,
watch me frown
these feelings are true.
When my spirits lift up
color me green,
that's my favorite color
when I'm tranquil and serene.
My moods sway as you can see
from angry to sad,
or happy as can be
currently I'm feeling glad.
It's Christmas glad tidings all around
play music I need to hear some Christmas sound,
color me blue, color me green
I love being happy and serene.

By Dennis Andrew Massei
12-25-2020

18.

Flowers

Look at the pretty flowers
beneath sunny skies so clear,
suddenly showers
a sure sign that spring is near.
Roses violets tulips and moms
it's a beautiful world when spring comes,
sun showers are not so drear
it's just a sign that spring is near.
After sun showers
it's a breath of fresh air,
and a garden of pretty flowers
the beauty is everywhere.
Pretty roses and other flowers too
beneath skies of blue
hyacinth is a favorite flower I hold dear and I can tell that
spring is here.

By Dennis Andrew Massei
12-31-2020

My first poem in 2021.

19.

God Bless the World
I Live in

God bless the world I live in,

may it be filled with peace and love,

and may it be free from sin,

that's all I'm thinking of.

If everybody thought like me,

what a beautiful world it would be,

I'll just keep praying again and again,

God bless the world I live in.

God bless my neighbors, friends or foe,

my soul's filled with kindness let it show,

we can all benefit and win,

God bless the world I live in.

God bless the world I live in,

as I pray again and again,

may it be free from sorrow and pain,

faith and love may we all regain.

Say a little prayer,

and know God is everywhere,

pray over and over again,
God bless the world I live in.

By Dennis Andrew Massei
01-02-2021

20.

A Heavenly Dream

I'm walking the streets of heaven in my dreams
wondering is it what it seems.
I really want to know
I don't want to awake
'cause I can't wait to go.
It's peace and quiet up there
no sounds of violence, protests filling the air.
Dirt roads lined with trees of green
One can really enjoy the scene.
Eternal peace is a treasure
living life full measure.
Back to reality as I awake
this is one dream I can take.

By Dennis Andrew Massei
1-2-2021

21.

Walking and Talking
with the Lord

I'm walking down a lonely highway
the Lord close by hears me pray,
I never knew till this day
he heard every prayer I prayed.
The road is no longer lonely with the Lord by my side
he forgives my sins and what I need he promised to provide.
I take into account each day and night
the Lord has blessed me well,
I'll always follow in his light
and praise his name to everyone I tell.
I worship him in public it's what he prefers me to do
for he is my friend loyal and true.
When I hear his voice in my head
I listen to every word being said.
He knows when I answer too
by my actions in the deeds I do.

By Dennis Andrew Massei
01-06-2021

22.

God's Two Greatest Gifts

I love the world I love life

my heart's filled with love in my soul there is peace,

end worldwide troubles and strife

and any violence let it cease.

Live life as full as a life can be

God gave this gift to you and me,

just don't waste it or throw it away

get out and enjoy it every single day.

Have fun now before it's too late

don't put it off and wait,

I could go on and on

one day your life will be gone.

I love life and I love the world too

two greatest gifts God made for me and you.

By Dennis Andrew Massei
01-08-2021

23.

Birth of a Poem

Sometimes I get an idea to write
in the wee hours of morning light,
the need to write down
these thoughts I get from all around,
very early in the morn
a brand-new poem is born.
An idea that comes from the sky
gazing at the sunrise,
or looking at the trees and grassy scenes
and things that look peaceful and serene.
Watching the sunset
while the sky's not too dark yet,
an idea could be beyond the stars
in heaven afar.
An idea may just appear there
they come from everywhere,
anytime evening or morn
A new poem is born.

By Dennis Andrew Massei
01-12-2021

24.

My Dream World

Any violence would have to cease
what follows next is peace,
a world of people coming together
being friendly with one another.
It is spring all year round
bees humming, birds singing, how cool does nature sound.
Introducing my dream world and it is my pleasure
where you can slow down to a walk live life full measure.
The sun shining after spring showers
and then they bloom, all the pretty flowers.
The smell of spring in the air
friendly people everywhere,
everybody knows your name
my dream world, I love it just the same.

By Dennis Andrew Massei
01-16-2021

25.

In God I Trust

If there's a problem anywhere,

I just sit there,

I don't worry or make a fuss,

because, in God I trust.

He's always been there in the past,

the problems I see never seem to last,

praying is a must,

because, in God I trust.

I don't put it off for too long,

I pray before something goes wrong,

I don't get angry I don't cuss,

it's just, in God I trust.

Dennis Andrew Massei

01-17-2021

26.
My Life

This picture of me when I was nine,
my childhood life seemed perfectly fine.
I had no worries to speak of,
just my family in a home filled with love.
I loved school but mostly I loved to play,
God sometimes I wish I can go back to my childhood and
stay.
Soon I'll turn fifty-nine,
my life is still pretty fine.
I still have my mother who's loving and caring,
and I take her love and be forever sharing.

By Dennis Andrew Massei
01-19-2021

27.

There's a Hero in My Heart

There's a hero in my heart
whom I've accepted from the start,
he accepted me for good behavior
Jesus Christ the almighty savior.
He is the man I most admire
to be in heaven someday is all I desire,
I worship as often as I can
and read my Bible that I might understand.
I praise his name everywhere
I kneel at the cross in prayer,
he is the hero I turn to
to fix the problems no one else can do,
a huge part of my life from the start
there's a hero in my heart.

By Dennis Andrew Massei
01-20-2021

28.

I Love to Tell the Story

I love to tell the story

of Jesus and his love,

a story of when he died that's sad and true

his death was not in vain for he died for me and you.

I love to tell the story

some people hated him others adored and loved,

those people shared his glory

and will dwell in Heaven above.

I love to tell the story

of Jesus and his love,

I'll be in all my glory

when I get to Heaven above.

By Dennis Andrew Massei
01-20-2021

29.
In My Own Little World

I live in my own little world
where all is peaceful and calm,
family and friends and all I can think of
in my own little world filled with love.
I live in my own little world
where it's sunny every day,
a passing shower or two
I live life my way
with my faith in God so true.
In my own little world, I get along
where nothing ever seems to go wrong,
born and raised in the USA
where a man can live life his way.
One proud American as happy as can be
in my own little world
I enjoy living free.

By Dennis Andrew Massei
01-22-2021

30.
Upon the Lord's Return

When the Lord comes back to Earth,
everything will be calm and still,
as he passes judgment on what our lives are worth,
in the air there might be a little chill.
Repent your sins now, I advise you not to wait,
for once he comes it might be too late.
We don't know when he's coming but we should be ready
in any case,
so, if we're selected for Heaven, we could promptly take
our place.
Do yourself a favor, head to your church to repent,
you'll be glad you went,
afterwards you may see angels in the sky.
It's great to save yourself before you die.

By Dennis Andrew Massei
01-24-2021

31.
I Lost My Daddy Long Ago

I lost my Daddy long ago,
and I want you all to know,
I miss him every day,
and love him more than words can say.
The timing of his passing was all wrong,
for sometimes I struggle along,
what I wanted to say while he was here,
the bond we shared I'll continue to cherish year after year.
He left us with no chance to say goodbye,
he left us too soon too young to die.
We're meet in Heaven someday,
and have lunch with Jesus in his home far away.
Just wanted you all to know,
I lost my daddy long ago.

By Dennis Andrew Massei
01-28-2021

32.
The Ghost Hiding Within Me

There's a ghost hiding within me,
years ago, I called him Dad,
'cause you see,
he was the best friend I ever had.
I walk like him and I talk like him too,
some folks say I even look like him and I think I do.
I can feel him sometimes peeking out of my eyes,
and then I tear up that's when I begin to cry.
When I open my mouth,
the ghost tries to climb out.
He's in my heart he's in my soul,
and everybody can see,
that's the ghost hiding within me.

By Dennis Andrew Massei
01-28-2021

33.
Listen to Me

Listen to what I am saying,

you got to fall on your knees and start praying.

You got to believe in God without any doubt,

listen to me, I know what I'm talking about.

I will repeat myself again,

if you will listen to me,

the Lord will forgive your sin,

and set you free.

His holy name you can praise and shout,

believe his holy word and erase any doubt.

Listen to me and do your part,

and believe with your whole heart,

believe beyond a shadow of a doubt,

listen to me, I know what I'm talking about.

By Dennis Andrew Massei
01-29-2021

34.

A Garden for Heaven

I'm planting a garden for Heaven planting seeds of good all
around, if evil comes knocking, I will face the devil down.
Helping people who needs
paying it forward by doing good deeds.
If my seeds are uprooted and evil stands it's ground, I will
face the devil down.
In my garden for Heaven
all my seeds have grown,
the devil is passing
my good deeds have been sown.
Seeds of good are planted all over town
all the good deeds I've done,
if everyone pays it forward
we can bring evil down.

By Dennis Andrew Massei
01-30-2021

35.
God is My Co-Pilot

No matter where I'm driving,
God occupies the seat beside me,
no matter where I'm arriving,
I've no more sins my soul is pure and free.
No matter what direction my life is going,
with God as my co-pilot,
I've got blessings overflowing.
God's love is multiplied,
for he is my co-pilot,
when my number is called,
in Heaven I won't be denied.
I'll praise his holy name forever
and forever I will see,
God as my co-pilot,
and my soul is forever free.

By Dennis Andrew Massei
02-04-2021

36.
The More I Repent

The more I repent
the stronger I feel
and my weaker side disappears
the secrets are out and so I reveal.
The more I repent
the stronger my will to live
my smile is Heaven sent
in all I may give.
The more I repent
the more I know
God's love
when he calls, I will go.
The more I repent
the more I see
God's will
to set me free.

By Dennis Andrew Massei
02-06-2021

37.
An Angel in My Heart

God put an angel in my heart
when the angel does its part,
soon I'll hear songs I love
sweet sounds from heaven above.
I love to hear angels singing
the joy they will be bringing,
I believed in angels right from the start
when God put an angel in my heart.
The angels I watch them fly
when I look up to the sky,
I know they're watching over me
they're sent from God his love I see.
Angels are miracles don't you know
if you believe it's Heaven you will go,
I've known this right from the start
when God put an angel in my heart.

By Dennis Andrew Massei
02-06-2021

38.

How I Trusted God

I trusted God all the days of my life
he saw me through my troubles and strife,
I'm sitting here today 'cause God loves me
he forgave my sins and set me free.
I'll always trust God with anything
'cause he knows my needs and he will bring,
that's why I keep God's love in my heart
and I've done so right from the start.
It's all I can do
is promise to be faithful and true,
through God I know
all things are possible and so
I pray to God everyday
that he will lead the way
forever and always
all the rest of my days.

By Dennis Andrew Massei
02/07/2021

39.
Nothing but Love in
My Heart

I've got nothing but love in my heart
from the time of my life at the start,
imagine if everybody thought like me
they'll be no hate in this world to see.
God send down some love for we cannot wait
put it in the hearts of those who hate,
live life full measure and let the world see your smile
life is not guaranteed for God only lent it for a while.
At the time of my death the world loses a lifetime of love,
for my reward I'll live eternally in Heaven above.

By Dennis Andrew Massei
02-13-2021

40.
If I Come to You Tomorrow

If I come to you tomorrow
would I pass the judgement test?
Would you ease my pain and sorrow
and give me some peace and rest?
As far as I know
my whole life I've been good,
if I'm called to go
did I do all I should?
I come to you 'cause you are the best
at easing pain and sorrow
and lending peace and rest
If I come to you tomorrow
may I enter in?
I'll be returning the life I borrowed
and to thank you
for forgiving my sin

By Dennis Andrew Massei
02-15-2021

41.

Oh Lord my God, I Saw the Light

With every passing year
I stop drinking beer,
I give beer up for lent
and all my sins I repent.
Just me and my savior
being on my best behavior,
trying hard to make things right
Oh Lord my God, I saw the light.
With God I make my peace
all my troubles will cease,
I'm trying as best I could
everything will be good.
I no longer walk in darkness
I'm walking the path of righteousness,
the road looks bright
Oh Lord my God, I saw the light.

By Dennis Andrew Massei
02-17-2021

42.

If You Believe

If the road of life seems wrong,

still sing a happy song,

if you have nothing to hide,

you'll walk with the Lord side by side.

Get it out in the open,

and clear the air,

someday you'll be welcomed in heaven,

and live forever in God's care.

Your sins will be forgiven,

despite the life you've been liven,

so, bow your head in prayer,

by the time you're done you'll see God standing there.

If you believe that God is real,

and you believe in what you feel,

you'll know it is true,

that God will always love you.

By Dennis Andrew Massei
02-18-2021

43.

My Journey of Life

As I travel along
each day of my life.
I can see, behind me
all my troubles and strife.
I used to think, my life was wrong
then suddenly,
everything looked clear and bright.
That's when Jesus came along
that's about the time
I saw the light.
Welcome to my journey
my journey of life
sometimes the road was smooth
sometimes it was rough.
In my troubles and strife
I thought I've had enough.
Then Jesus showed me the way
in this life of mine

I'm praying with each new day
and everything now is fine.

By Dennis Andrew Massei
02-24-2021

44.
Jesus and Me

I made my peace with Jesus long ago,
there's something you should all come to know,
going to church isn't enough,
you gotta be tough,
face the devil down,
spread good deeds all around.
Every minute of each new day,
live your life like Jesus all the way,
never let your guard down,
be always happy never show a frown.
Spread the holy word,
let your voice be heard,
I made my piece with Jesus long ago,
sometimes I still wonder so,
about the powers that be,
when I talk to Jesus,
it's just Jesus and me.

By Dennis Andrew Massei
02-25-2021

45.

I Can See the Light of Day

I can see the light of day
in the darkest part of night,
I will follow down the highway
that is lighted so bright.
I can see our precious savior
in all his glory and might,
nothing stands in the way
of me and the light.
I can see the light of day
in the darkest part of night,
I see our precious savior
from all walks of life,
caring for those mired in troubles and strife.
A hero through his mercy and might
in the darkest part of night,
I can see the light of day
as I follow along the way.

By Dennis Andrew Massei
02-26-2021

46.

I See God Everywhere

I see God everywhere,
oh, I'm not complaining,
I feel good knowing he is there.
Before I go to sleep at night,
I say a little prayer,
then I turn out the light,
and realize I rely on God's care.
As I'm awaken to greet a new day,
again, you'll hear me pray,
thanking him for being there,
I see God everywhere.
Live life full and live it well,
some words to live by I do tell,
my love too I'd like to share,
I see God everywhere.
In my heart and in my soul,
in my mind I set my goal,
in my house and in my car,
in the sky I see heaven afar.
in the sunshine and in the rain,
he will heal all your pain.

He is here he is there,
I see God everywhere.

By Dennis Andrew Massei
02-27-2021

47.

A Song in My Heart

There's a song in my heart,
a song of
Jesus' love,
and the good things
that come from heaven above.
Stomp the devil's face in the ground,
may peace and love reign all around,
let evil play no part,
of a song in my heart.
I will always believe,
sorrow and pain he'll relieve,
God is love right from the start,
as I sing a song in my heart.
Ask for anything you shall receive,
if you believe,
miracles plays its part,
as I sing a song in my heart.
Good things come to those who wait,
blessings are never late,

till this life I depart,
I'll sing a song in my heart.

By Dennis Andrew Massei
02-27-2021

48.

I Wanna be a Poem Star

I wanna be a poem star
I write things all the time
I write about things how they are,
I love to make words rhyme.
I like to write about God,
and some are about me,
whatever's on my mind
while I'm feeling humble and free.
This is who I am,
It's how I pass the time,
I'll make a song and jam,
I love to make words rhyme.
I wanna be known the world over,
I want everyone to know my name,
Now remember Dennis Andrew Massei,
his quest for worldwide fame.

By Dennis Andrew Massei

49.
The Story of God to Me

Well, the story of God to me,
is the best I've ever known,
it's pretty clear I see,
the Bible's the best book I own.
The words printed in red,
that's what God had said,
say your prayers and be prepared,
in the Bible the scriptures were shared.
This is what they say,
upon God's return is judgment day,
through the son of God I believe,
all our sins were relieved.
I cannot help the way I feel,
the Bible is true and real,
it's pretty clear I see,
The story of God to me.

By Dennis Andrew Massei
03-04-2021

50.
Fitted for My Wings

When I was a small boy,
I was fitted for my wings,
'cause God saw the joy,
to most other kids I bring.
Behaving as every kid should,
no matter what evil brings,
God saw I always made good,
so, he fitted me for my wings.
Even now as I'm a grown-up man,
I still try as best I can,
to look for good in all bad things,
So, God fitted me for my wings.
In everything I do,
I search for the good things,
my intentions are true,
as I get fitted for my wings.

By Dennis Andrew Massei
03-10-2021

51.
Will You

Will you act the way you should
in good faith to do good?
Or will you stumble along
doing things you know are wrong?
If you see God by your side
will you accept him or run and hide?
If you knew in advance
that you will win
and were given a chance
to live your life over again.
Will you have learned to live right?
Will you follow Jesus day and night?
Whether your sins are too many or few
miracles still happen right on cue.
Will you accept Jesus as your friend?
In your journey to the end.
Eternal peace begins life anew
when your earthly life is through.

By Dennis Andrew Massei
03-11-2021

52.
Season of Spring

Flowers are blooming everywhere,
the scent of spring is in the air.
Beneath the deep blue skies,
the sun is shining in your eyes.
Take it outside and stay awhile,
put on your best springtime smile.
It's a feel good kinda season,
it makes me wanna sing,
I've got a real good reason,
just because it's spring.
Plant a rose then plant a tree,
something beautiful soon we'll see.
What's next for mother nature to bring,
the beauty of it all this season of spring.
What I'm feeling in my heart,
it's a beautiful thing,
as mother nature plays her part,
in the season of spring.

By Dennis Andrew Massei
03-12-2021

53.

When Jesus Calls

When Jesus calls,
you better answer,
and clearly state your case,
if you don't answer,
in his kingdom, he may deny your place.
When Jesus calls,
say hi how are you
in a friendly kind of way,
when Jesus calls,
tell him you've been loyal and true,
and you praise his name each day.
When Jesus calls,
don't be discouraged
if you haven't behaved your best,
when Jesus calls,
show your courage,
for he promised eternal rest.
When Jesus calls
and you accept him,
he'll welcome you in
to thy kingdom,

when Jesus calls
to forgive your sins.

By Dennis Andrew Massei
03-19-2021

54.

It's a Beautiful World to Me

As I glance around
and let nothing get me down.
I look straight ahead as far as my eyes can see,
it's a beautiful world to me.
Looking past the evil things,
focusing only on the good,
look up and observe the beauty heaven brings,
I'd stay here a hundred years if I could.
On a clear day
for miles I can see,
Look straight up and far away,
it's a beautiful world to me.
Even if the day is gray
look past the evil that stands in the way,
love conquers all and it is free,
it's a beautiful world to me.

By Dennis Andrew Massei
03-22-2021

55.

I Come to you My Friend

I've followed Jesus early on,
in my life it's an ongoing trend,
when I have a problem Jesus,
I come to you, my friend.
All at once it seems things go wrong,
in my struggles to get along,
when I reach my wits end,
Jesus, I come to you, my friend.
Eventually things turn out right,
I owe it all to a time I saw the light,
worship service I attend,
Jesus, I come to you, my friend.
In heaven I believe I've earned my place,
someday Jesus we'll meet face to face,
at that time my earthly life shall end,
Jesus, I come to you, my friend.

By Dennis Andrew Massei
03-28-2021

56.

I am Never Alone

My family and friends I dearly love,
among them I'm constantly thinking of.
Jesus Christ, the greatest friend of all,
he is always there when I call.
Long ago when I saw the light,
I began praying morning, noon and night.
The owner of my life is clearly known,
It's Jesus Christ and I am never alone.
Each prayer that I pray
that's how I make the call,
an image that I see each day,
It was Jesus Christ I saw.
Every day he walks by my side,
anything I need he sure does provide.
For he's the greatest friend I've ever known,
that's Jesus Christ and I am never alone.

By Dennis Andrew Massei
04-01-2021

57.

When God Makes the Call

For all the good within my life,
I've had my share of troubles and strife.
Jesus made me all better made me alright,
all because I saw the light.
Jesus is in my heart and in my soul,
and I'm building my home in heaven
setting my heavenly goal.
I'm living right as opposed to wrong,
my world is bright as I try to get along.
As the day I was born, I'll go back to being pure,
in that world in eternal life when I reach Heaven's shore,
in this world in this life the beauty of it all,
I'm heading to Heaven when God makes the call.

By Dennis Andrew Massei
04-08-2021

58.

My Savior and Me

What have I done to deserve such love,
from the savior in heaven above.
As I say again, I repent my sin.
For all the times I prayed
I'll be saved come judgement day.
All the things that are good and kind,
are what's on my mind.
What's in my heart, but
the goodness which feeds my soul,
my savior has a part,
fulfilling my every goal.
Look deep into my eyes
a path to my soul you'll find,
How I passed the test
in too many tries,
boggles my mind.
My heart is sincere for sure
deep inside you can see,

a portrait, of a life so pure
a picture of, my savior and me.

By Dennis Andrew Massei
04-13-2021

59.

When Jesus Befriended Me

At a time in my life
in my troubles and strife
when I felt down and out
and wondered what life was about.
Like nothing I've ever seen
my sins were wiped clean
my soul was set free
when Jesus befriended me.
Now I'm living right
because I saw the light
I worship and I pray
each and every day.
Since I've grown from boy to man
I've come to understand
Jesus' troubles greater than mine
when he died to make my life fine.
I'm so happy to be free
when Jesus befriended me.

By Dennis Andrew Massei
04-17-2021

60.
Remembering My Dad

I'll never forget that sad day
when my dad went away up to heaven he went
my heart was all broken and bent.
Why so young did my dad die?
Without a chance to say good-bye.
I will always love and miss my dad
the best friend I ever had.
My memories of years ago
the good old days I use to know
I was a little boy wild and free
I liked to bounce on daddy's knee.
Sometimes we'd go out for a walk or stayed home to sit and talk.
Remembering those days with my dad, just makes me feel less sad.

By Dennis Andrew Massei

61.
Mother Nature and Me

It's a beautiful world I see just mother nature and me,
skies of blue trees of green out in the country peaceful and
serene.
My cabin by the road on a little hill
a peaceful night all is calm and still,
up and out early on my nature walk
listening to the birds in their chirping talk.
Sunrise, sunset in summer and fall
appreciate the beauty of it all,
autumn leaves turn brown
as they come down,
as the leaves hit the ground, hear the dry, crinkly sound.
Out in the country my favorite place to be
just mother nature and me.

By Dennis Andrew Massei
11-21-2019

62.

My Faith on the Line

When I'm down and feeling blue

I think God loves me true,

then I know there's nothing I can't do with God guiding me
through.

In my struggles to get along

I realize God will never lead me wrong, as I put my faith on
the line

suddenly everything works out fine.

Since I've come to know God and his son

I've had my sins deleted one by one,

at the cross one day is where I saw the light, since then I've
been living right.

God and his son are two of my greatest friends although
there were temptations I've proved to resist, our friendship
will last long after my life ends, without them, I could never
exist.

By Dennis Andrew Massei
04-18-2021

63.
Many Heroes

I've had many heroes throughout my life
they helped me through my troubles and strife
first there were my mother and my dad
who dried away my tears when something made me sad.
Two sets of grandparents who loved me so
teaching me things I needed to know.
My aunts and uncles influenced me too
whose advice helped me decide what I needed to do.
The pastor who told me what I needed to hear
about Jesus Christ who loves me dear
from that moment on I stood tall
when Jesus Christ forgave my sins,
he became my greatest hero of all.

By Dennis Andrew Massei
04-19-2021

64.

I'm Trudging Along

I don't want to lose him
no, I don't want to hide
so, I'm trudging along
with Jesus by my side.
If I find myself lagging behind
about to lose my way
he eases my troubled mind
with these words I heard him say.
Keep trudging along
it doesn't matter your speed
I'm always near you
to provide whatever you need.
I try the best I can
to keep up and be strong
Jesus is always near me
I knew it all along.

By Dennis Andrew Massei
04-20-2021

65.

Lord Jesus Take My Hand

I need a new place to roam
Lord Jesus take my hand
and guide me safely home
to your kingdom in heaven land.
When my life shall cease
and I am at peace
tucked safely beneath an angel's wing
on my way to that heavenly spring.
I'll meet my maker face to face
in my heavenly place
I'll be with my loved ones up there
in God's tender care.
God's kingdom in heaven land
I'll have a new place to roam
Lord Jesus take my hand
and lead me home.

By Dennis Andrew Massei
04-20-2021

66.
My Fondest Wish

Grant my fondest wish Lord I pray,
allow my life to reach a hundred years and a day.
My prayers get answered
immediately after I pray,
and I hear him reply
these words he did say.
Come unto me my son,
as your sins get erased one by one.
To my heart I've asked him in,
he forgave my every sin,
just like he promised he'd do,
now my life's as good as new.
Though my eyes may fill with tears,
as I grow into my twilight years,
I swear on my heart as pure as gold,
I'll pray for good health when I'm old.
My fondest wish to live a hundred years or so,
if it's granted Lord somehow let me know.

When it's time Lord take my hand,
lead me on to the promised land.

By Dennis Andrew Massei
04-22-2021

67.

Sunshine

Sunshine so pretty in the sky,
in summer and spring,
creates a sparkle in my eye,
and the flowers in the ground,
happiness all around,
the beauty sunshine can bring.
In a warm summer breeze,
birds are singing in the trees,
it's evident mother nature came to play,
this warm and sunny day.
In a park nearby,
kids are playing and having fun,
flying a kite so high in the sky,
under the afternoon sun.
I love all four seasons,
Spring, summer winter and fall,
I've got a hundred thousand reasons,
to enjoy the beauty of them all.

By Dennis Andrew Massei
04-23-2021

68.
Pretty Pictures

Pretty pictures of me in my youth,

remembering me from ages seven through ten,

to tell you the truth,

I loved myself back then.

Shame we can't turn back time,

if only for a little while,

back in my younger days,

I had a pretty smile.

Now I'm middle aged and a little passed my prime,

been treated well by father time,

I still have a heart of gold,

I look pretty good and I don't feel very old.

Pretty pictures are precious to me,

at a time when I was wild and free,

I loved myself when I was young and small,

Those are the greatest pictures of all.

By Dennis Andrew Massei
04-24-2021

69.

In the Face of Evil

In the face of evil,

I'll stand my ground,

with Jesus in my corner,

protecting me from all around.

There's no way I'll be defeated,

for Jesus will help me win,

the strength of all evil will be depleted,

I'll stand tall and proud again.

In the face of evil,

be good and kind,

love will conquer all,

believe it in your mind.

The war between good and evil seems will never end,

but one thing is for certain,

in the face of evil,

Jesus is your best friend.

By Dennis Andrew Massei

04-24-2021

70.

When I Drink a Beer

When I drink a beer
I feel full of cheer
for a little while
I feel myself smile.
I drink a beer or two
when my eyes are filled with tears
I feel happy temporarily
and my sadness disappears.
When the beer wears off
I find what made me sad
my troubles are still there
no matter how many beers I had.
I can't forget no matter how hard I try
beer is only a temporary solution
for things that make me cry.
It's just an allusion
but Jesus Christ is real
so, I turn to prayer

oh, how good I feel,
my friend Jesus Christ is there.

By Dennis Andrew Massei

04-25-2021

71.

In My Heart

In my heart, Jesus lives,
many blessings he gives.
In my heart, that's pure as gold,
I believe his truth I was told.
In my heart, I can feel,
his love that's true and real.
In my heart, is all my love,
I share to all who are worthy of.
In my heart, my faith is strong,
yes, I believe and I'm getting along.
In my heart, I can hear,
his voice is plain and clear.
In my heart, Jesus is calling me,
to my soul,
where he set me free.

By Dennis Andrew Massei
04-27-2021

72.

The Blues

If the blues, are realigned,
with my heart, and assigned.
To destroy, my will to live,
and all, I have to give.
I'll fall down, on my knees and pray,
before I go, to my home far away.
I'll muddled through, and get by,
because, it's not my wish to die.
I've got the blues, worst I've ever known,
wish these blues, leave me alone.
Lord, heal my troubled mind,
I want to leave, the blues behind.
Precious Lord, take my hand,
tell me what, you've got planned.
My blues, filled heart is on the mend,
thanks, to Jesus my one true friend.

By Dennis Andrew Massei
04-29-2021

No, I'm not depressed or feeling low down, but merely inspired by Hank William's Sr. songs of the lonesome sound.

73.
Hooked on Jesus

I am hooked on Jesus
but it's perfectly alright
if I have to be hooked on someone
I'm glad it's Jesus day and night.
I mention his name at least once
in every poem I write
that's how I praise his name
may I shine forever in his light.
I am hooked on Jesus
I stand tall and proud
to write his name in my poem
then I'll praise his name aloud.
It's perfectly fine
to have a talent like mine
It's a big plus
to have a friend like him
I'm hooked on Jesus.

By Dennis Andrew Massei
04-30-2021

74.

If Jesus Comes Tomorrow

If Jesus comes tomorrow
would you know you are gone?
If you have no pain or sorrow
would you let him guide you
as you walk on?
If Jesus comes tomorrow
will you feel lost and alone?
Would you cry in sorrow
if your fate is not known?
If Jesus comes tomorrow
will you feel good and strong?
Did you know all along
you'll be accepted at the throne?
If Jesus comes tomorrow
and your fate is fully known
you will not be alone
as Jesus leads you home.

By Dennis Andrew Massei
05-01-2021

75.

I'm Satisfied with My Life as Is

I'm satisfied with
my life as is.
I'm not real sad
just a little blue.
I'm not real happy
just a little cheery
all I desire
is some jewelry
a little silver too
maybe some gold
that'll be fine
all I want is
a little wealth to call mine.
I'm satisfied with
my life as is
I'd be contented
with a little house
to call my own
not real big though
but not too small
I don't need a mansion
just a little house is all.

I'm satisfied with
my life as is
don't call me rich
'cause I'm a little poor
If I had some wealth
I wouldn't ask for more.
I'm satisfied with
my life as is.
I may be poor
but I'm proud
of the things I've got
my life could be worse
but thank God it's not.
I'm satisfied with
my life as is.

By Dennis Andrew Massei
05-03-2021

76.
Master of the Blues

I've been lonely long enough
I've stood tall and hung tough,
There seems to be
nobody for me,
Lord I've paid my dues
now they call me,
master of the blues.
What I'm constantly thinking of
how I need a woman's love,
Lucky lady let's walk down the aisle
our love will have infinite miles.
Please come accept my heart
and pledge the vow till death we part,
these thoughts always on my mind
'cause true love is hard to find,
Put together all the clues
I am, master of the blues.

By Dennis Andrew Massei
05-07-2021

Another poem inspired by the late great Hank Williams Sr.

77.
It's a Grand Old Time
to Get Religion

It's a grand old time to get religion
walk into your church today
make your peace with God
don't let this chance slip away.
Talk to your minister
it's a good place to start
he'll have a prayer with you
and bring Jesus to your heart.
If you're feeling guilty for your sins
there's no reason to feel any shame
Glory be to Jesus
praise his holy name.
Wherever you are
fall on your knees and pray
it's a grand old time to get religion
Jesus will be there for you each day.

By Dennis Andrew Massei
05-07-2021

78.

How Far is Heaven

How far is heaven
I want to go
visit my father
he went there long ago.
how far is heaven
I'm feeling blue
'cause I miss him dearly
and I love him too.
How far is heaven
daddy turn on a light
I wanna see you
may I come tonight.
How far is heaven
I want to go
visit my father
'cause I miss him so.

By Dennis Andrew Massei
05-08-2021

79.

My Blessings are Easy
to Find

I don't see the devil

I suppress evil from my mind,

I only see good things

my blessings are easy to find.

Lord, please bless our schools

and the children too,

bless the good people,

who still have faith in you.

I don't see the devil

I suppress evil from my mind,

I only see good things,

my blessings are easy to find.

So, bless my family and my friends,

give them strength to defend their land,

give them justice, and may victory, be theirs in the end.

I don't see the devil

I suppress evil from my mind,

I only see good things,
my blessings, are easy to find.

By Dennis Andrew Massei
05-09-2021

80.

What Would the World Look Like When I'm Gone

Will my neighborhood look the same?

Like when I first came,

will this still be here?

What I've held dear,

will that still be there?

If I'm gone, I won't care.

But I wonder, what would the world look like when I'm gone?

Will people cry in sorrow 'cause I've passed on?

The places I used to roam,

to me, it was like being home.

Where I'm at today,

what was it like before I came?

Was it here way back then?

Is it different or the same?

After I've passed on,

what would the world look like when I'm gone?

By Dennis Andrew Massei

05-10-2021

81.

Face in the Sky

A question I ponder often
why my father had to die
he was much too young
every time I look up
I see a face in the sky.
I can feel him looking around
he knows when I'm sad and blue
he knows when I'm feeling down
I think he knows I miss him too.
He left us suddenly so soon
in some hours in the afternoon,
every time I look up
I see a face in the sky.
He knows when I'm happy
and he knows when I'm in tears
I can sense his spirit near me
though he's been gone many years.
My feelings I cannot conceal
for his love I still feel,
I know he sees me waving goodbye

every time I look up
I see a face in the sky.

By Dennis Andrew Massei
05-11-2021

82.
Forever Slumber

The Lord will call my number
when my home in heaven's completed,
there I'll forever slumber,
as my life on earth's deleted.
Till then I'll live my life happy
sometimes there's sorrow,
I know my time's coming
for my life I only borrowed.
My home is built in heaven
from my actions in this life,
it's earned by good deeds I do
and my own troubles and strife.
So, Lord when you're ready for me
you have my number,
call and I will be
home shortly to forever slumber.

By Dennis Andrew Massei
05-12-2021

83.

A Stairwell to Heaven

I'm going up to heaven
for a little while
to visit my dad
I want to see him smile
I miss him real bad.
There's a stairwell to heaven
next to the rainbow
the Lord makes it easy
whenever I want to go.
Up, up and around the bend
seems this stairwell has no end,
up and around again and again
until I'm all in.
I'm on my way to heaven
to visit my dad
I'll be back in a little while
when I'm over being sad.

By Dennis Andrew Massei
05-13-2021

84.

The Beauty in Heaven

It never rains in heaven
the sun is shining there
it's neither hot nor humid
just cool, gentle heavenly air.
There's no old buildings in heaven
no eye sores to stare
no stench of the city
only fresh heavenly air.
No cracks on the streets of heaven
no graffiti on the walls there
nothing but heaven's beauty
for your eyes to stare.
It isn't too cold there
in heaven it never snows
for the garden, some fresh air
beauty is all that heaven knows.

By Dennis Andrew Massei
05-19-2021

85.
What's in a Friday

What's in a Friday
besides the end
of a busy week,
a little r and r is
all I seek.
I'll lose myself
in my writing
I may be hard to find,
this is what happens
with a poem on my mind.
This r and r
that I need writing
poems relaxes me,
to complete a poem
then how proud I be.
I love to share, my poems there,
for all to see,
now there's no one
more relaxed as me.
What's in a Friday
but a weekend gone too fast,
another Friday now in the past.

Before long Monday's here
my heart's full of cheer,
time to get back to the grind
now I'll make myself easy to find.

By Dennis Andrew Massei
05-20-2021

86.
My Savior and Me

What have I done to deserve such love
from the savior in heaven above
as I say again, I repent my sin,
for all the times I prayed
I'll be saved come judgement day.
All the things that are good and kind
are what's on my mind
what's in my heart
but the goodness which feeds my soul
my savior has a part
fulfilling my every goal.
Look deep into my eyes
a path to my soul you'll find
how I passed the test
in too many tries
boggles my mind.
My heart is sincere for sure
deep inside you can see

a portrait, of a life so pure
a picture of, my savior and me.

By Dennis Andrew Massei

04-13-2021

87.
Have You Ever Wondered

Have you ever wondered
where your faith lies,
or where you're going
when you die.
You gotta believe in God
believe in your heart,
Jesus was your friend
from the start.
So, make your peace with God
come join me at church today,
we'll take communion
then kneel at the cross and pray.
Take the first step
before it's too late,
repent your sins now why wait?
One day you will be
knocking at heaven's door,
and not unlike me
we'll live with Christ evermore.

By Dennis Andrew Massei
05-22-2021

88.

The Love of My Life

The love of my life
hails from a faraway land
I don't mind telling you
he's my buddy man to man.
A certain power comes over me
every time I pray
and the blessings I receive
every single day.
When something goes wrong
suddenly it turns out alright
so, I'm getting along
and the future is looking bright.
If you believe my story is true
I'm pretty sure he's your friend too.
I think now you understand
the love of my life is God
and he hails from heaven
in that faraway land.

By Dennis Andrew Massei
05-23-2021

89.

A Lost Soul Without a Home

In the new world up there

I hope I'm not left to roam

I'd rather be in God's care

than to be, a lost soul without a home.

I hope I pass the test

when it's time to forever rest,

I'm sure my fate was always known

I won't be, a lost soul without a home.

For all the good I've done

I've earned my chance to meet God's son,

the greatest friend I've known

I won't be, a lost soul without a home.

If I've earned any here

give me a place to call my own,

I've always kept Jesus near

so I wouldn't be, a lost soul without a home.

By Dennis Andrew Massei
05-27-2021

90.
Christmas Season

I'm getting a jump on Christmas
it'll be here before you know,
this year's flying by
okay here I go.
I'm putting up my nativity scene
I'll wait awhile to put up my tree,
peaceful and serene
is how everyday should be.
I can't ask for anything more
in my favorite time of year,
Jesus is the reason we do this for
and the children, so happy full of cheer.
Let me be in my glory
getting set for Christmas season,
I can tell a story
of how Jesus became the reason.

By Dennis Andrew Massei
05-27-2021

91.

Good Hearted Man

I love to give my help
to anyone who needs
this is who I am
I love to do good deeds.
I will always be there
to lend a helping hand
believe me when I say I care
I'm a good-hearted man.
I'm a good listener
the very best,
if anything, you'd like to say
and get it off your chest.
To bring you some cheer
that is my plan,
I am always here
I'm a good-hearted man.

By Dennis Andrew Massei
05-28-2021

92.
Jesus is Coming

Jesus is coming
to a church near you,
he's bringing friendship
and loyalty true.
Your sins be forgiven
forgotten and gone,
Jesus is coming with promise
your life lives on and on.
Jesus is coming
he'll judge you at that time,
whether you go with him
how serious your crime.
Jesus is coming
he loves us all so dear,
I often had a feeling
he was always near.

By Dennis Andrew Massei
05-28-2021

93.
That's the Jesus Christ
I Know

The Jesus Christ that I know
is good loyal and true,
he unburdened our sorrows and woes
in spite of the sins we do.
He's a friend who's not hard to find
for he is everywhere,
he can heal what's on your troubled mind
through his love and merciful care.
His friendship is one I love to cling to
it is the greatest one I own,
and no matter what I do
I know I'm never alone.
Take Jesus by the hand
and never let go,
he's a friend you can understand
that's the Jesus Christ I know.

By Dennis Andrew Massei
05-29-2021

94.

I See God Everywhere

I see God everywhere
oh, I'm not complaining
I feel good knowing he is there.
Before I go to sleep at night
I say a little prayer
then I turn out the light
and realize I rely on God's care.
As I'm awakened to greet a new day
again, you'll hear me pray
thanking him for being there
I see God everywhere.
Live life full and live it well
some words to live by I do tell
my love too I'd like to share
I see God everywhere.
In my heart and in my soul
in my mind I set my goal
in my house and in my car
in the sky I see heaven afar
in the sunshine and in the rain
he will heal all your pain.

He is here he is there
I see God everywhere.

By Dennis A. Massei
aka Denny Dymes
02-27-2021

95.

Jesus' Love I Will Never Trade

I would never trade Jesus' love
no, not at any price,
someday I wanna go to heaven above
so, I gotta behave pleasant and nice.
He gives me strength to do my deeds
then provides for my needs,
he helped me with things I handmade
no, these blessings I will never trade.
He put love in my heart
and made me nice through to my soul,
I wanna stay this way till this life I part
by the time I die I hope I reach my goal.
He keeps me all together
for my life was heaven made,
I will cherish his love forever
Jesus' love I will never trade,
no Jesus' love I will never trade.

By Dennis Andrew Massei
06-06-2021

96.
Wanna Live a Little

Before it's my time to die
I don't want to just get by,
I want to live a little
before my bones are old and brittle.
I just want a little wealth
before I turn old and
I wanna live comfortable
before I'm lying still.
Turn me loose, show me some fun
lose my burdens, they weigh a ton.
Let me live a little bit
the hard times, I'd like to forget.
I wanna live a little
before I'm old and gray,
I appeal to my savior
hear me pray.

By Dennis Andrew Massei
06-07-2021

97.
You'll Always Know

Jesus called me today
just when I was about to pray,
says everything is good
and I've done all I could.
His voice was plain and clear
when he said, "I've got a job for you up here,"
"tell your family you're going away
there's no more need to pray."
I've been good and true
but what was I to do?
The savior called on me
and my soul he set free.
My heart is all aglow
now it's time for me to go,
we'll meet again someday
when it's your time to fly away.
One thing is for sure though
you'll always know,
when life is near the end
you realize Jesus is your friend.
When you're feeling tired and weary
and everything seems slow,

you're not feeling too cheery
your life is over, you'll always know.

By Dennis Andrew Massei
06-21-2021

129

98.

To Earn My Wings in Advance

If I'm given the chance
to earn my wings in advance
my sins will be gone
when I pass on.
I'll enter heaven
as an angel first class
I've planned this with my pastor at mass.
That's why I like to help
anybody who needs
I'll give all I can give
by doing good deeds.
If I fail to achieve my goal
dear Lord have mercy
on my immortal soul.
It was not my intent, Lord
to do you wrong
for I've tried my best
to do good and stay strong.
I thank the good people who needs
for allowing me to perform my good deeds

and giving me a chance
to earn my wings in advance.

By Dennis Andrew Massei
06-22-2021

99.
When Jesus Comes to Lead Me Home

Whenever I pass on
tell everyone I've gone,
take me to church
and make it known,
Jesus came to lead me home.
Take my poems
and let the world see,
money's no good in heaven
so, make them free.
I want the world to know
what I used to do,
take my poems, let the words flow
I wrote pretty good poems
but nobody knew.
Don't let my poems die in vain
publish them, make them known
let my legacy remain
when Jesus comes to lead me home.

By Dennis Andrew Massei06-27-2021

100.
Happy Friday

I like work
the weekend's near
I love Friday,
when it's over
time for some beer.
O happy Friday
I love to say,
it comes but once a week
two days rest is what we seek.
Gloomy Monday don't be sad
back to work it's not that bad,
I'll do the best I could
as the Lord makes this day good.

By Dennis Andrew Massei
06-25-2021

101.

I Know I'm Going to Heaven Someday

I know I'm going to Heaven someday,
I've lived in hell on earth,
dear Lord as often as I pray,
I'll never regret my birth.
Many crimes being committed,
violence never seems to end,
my repentance of sins, Lord, to you I've submitted,
proud to call you my friend.
I know I'm going to heaven someday,
it's hell on earth and I can't stay,
I've accepted Jesus a long time ago,
I should renew myself I know.
When I was a young boy,
things looked mighty good to me,
I only remember the fun and joy,
no evil did I see.
I know I'm going to heaven someday,
Jesus, there's no greater friend as he,

as I kneel down and pray,
I wish things were like they used to be.

By Dennis Andrew Massei
06-25-2021

102.

I Wanna Pack My Things and Move to Heaven

I wanna pack my things and move to heaven,

a place where crime and violence don't exist,

there's no pain or sorrow in heaven,

a place no one can resist.

I wanna pack my things and move to heaven,

where peace is normal every day,

criminals don't exist in heaven,

where all are welcome to stay.

I wanna pack my things and move to heaven,

a place where no soul is left behind,

everyone makes it into heaven,

no matter how big the burden troubling your mind.

I wanna pack my things and move to heaven,

a place in a land far away,

there's ample room in heaven,

for family and friends to come and stay.

By Dennis Andrew Massei
06-26-2021

103.
Dad's Shadow

He picks me up
when I fall down
it's great to know
he's still around.
I can see
Dad's shadow
looking after me
wherever I go.
It's been years
since he's gone
I still have tears
that linger on.
Tears, that never dry
Dad, why'd you go
why'd you have to die?
At least I can see, Dad's shadow.

By Dennis Andrew Massei
07-04-2021

Anthony P. Massei Jr.
January 30, 1936–October 17, 1991

104.
Comfy Little Fly

Gotta love this little fly's charm
when he lands on your arm.
His movements tickle you so
you don't want the fly to go.
He thinks you're trying to swat it
no, you love that little guy,
for when he lands on your arm
he's one comfy little fly.
Now he's buzzing around your head
afraid you want him dead,
you wait for him to land again
shaking your head with big wide grin.
Out the window he flew
and right on cue,
it's time to say goodbye
to that comfy little fly.

By Dennis Andrew Massei
06-27-2021

105.
God is Good, God is Great

God is good
God is great
for all he's done
I'll always appreciate.
He is my God
I worship only one
I'm proud to praise the name
of his only son.
I'll walk on streets of gold
in heaven some glad day
the treasures I hold
no longer come into play.
I'll praise his name
in my dying breath
it'll cause me no shame
as I close my eyes in death.

By Dennis Andrew Massei
06-30-2021

106.
I'm for God

All the joy
all the love
I'm a boy
born in heaven above.
I'm for God
and I believe
all my sins
he'll relieve.
I'm for God
as you heard before
stay faithful and true
you will live forever more.
I'm for God
it's plain to see
all the goodness
he gives for free.

By Dennis Andrew Massei
06-30-2021

107.
Jesus in My Heart

My heart is full of cheer
'cause I know Jesus is near.
My commitment to him I make
when he allows me to awake.
Jesus gave me the power
to be strengthened every hour
and my heart is all aglow
as I get up and go.
He is my savior
I'm honored and I'm proud
to go out in public
and praise his name aloud.
This is who I am
from the day I got my start
I will always welcome
Jesus in my heart.

By Dennis Andrew Massei
07-01-2021

108.

A Rainbow of People

Many colors
many races
a rainbow of people
all their pretty faces.
Coming together
like harmony and song
forming friendships
as they get along.
This is my dream world
I wish it to be true
we can live together
'cause God wants us to.
A rainbow of people
coming together
making friendships
like no other.
A rainbow of people
getting along

this is America
we're people strong.

By Dennis Andrew Massei
07-02-2021

109.
God be My Savior

God be my savior
I've been good you know
the sins of my past
you let them go.
God be my savior
I saw the light
the goodness you provide
are within my sight.
God be my savior
every day of my life
you got me through
if I had troubles and strife.
God be my savior
don't ever leave me be
stay within my heart and soul
and always keep me free.

By Dennis Andrew Massei
07-03-2021

110.
Happy Independence Day

My freedoms I appreciate
as we celebrate,
Independence Day
bar-b-que and games to play.
Two hundred and forty-five years
too many tears
shed for those who died
defending our freedoms
though they tried.
The National Anthem
sing our song
loud and clear
proudly sing along.
Raise our flag
raise it high
respect our soldiers
those who served
and those who died.
Here in America
God bless the USA
the land I love
Happy Independence Day.

God bless the USA
on land and on sea
I love America, home of the brave
land of the free.

By Dennis Andrew Masse
07-03-2021

111.
There's a Show Going on in Heaven

There's a show going on in heaven
a show of angels doing good,
they fly high in the sky
as we do the best we could.
Angels make miracles happen
all you gotta do is pray,
God will send the angels down
on any given day.
One day we'll all join the show
when we're through with our lives below,
we'll do a miracle on someone we love
or someone well thought of.
There's a show going on in heaven
a show that never ends
as the angels fly over you
you'll be forever friends.

By Dennis Andrew Massei
07-05-2021

112.
When the Blues Come Around

When the blues come around
you'll all come to know,
I'll be feeling lowest down
when the blues come around.
It happens about once each week
and it makes my life seem bleak,
I hear that lonesome sound,
when the blues come around.
I'll enjoy happy times
while they're here,
always know
that's when God is near.
I claimed God to be
my one true friend,
and I'll no longer feel low down
when the blues come around.

By Dennis Andrew Massei

07-05-2021

Inspired once again from the great works of the late Hank Williams Sr.

113.

I Will Go Away

I will go away
I will go away
they'll be a new place to roam.
I will go away
someday I'll fly away
to my heavenly home.
You'll have nothing to fear
so don't be scared my friend,
Jesus Christ is here
to guide you through
your journey's end.
I will go away
I will go away
they'll be a new place to roam.
I will go away
someday I'll fly away
to my heavenly home.
My life is owned
by a savior I've known,
he told me my fate
is death as I wait.
I will go away

I will go away
they'll be a new place to roam.
I will go away
someday I'll fly away
to my heavenly home.
In a new place I'll roam
when Jesus comes,
to lead me home.

By Dennis Andrew Massei
07-06-2021

114.
It's Too Hot for Me

The sun is shining outside
it's humid and hard to breathe,
I need relief, rain I hope will provide
it's too hot for me.
Mother Nature
take your humidity
pack your bags and go,
I prefer moderate temperatures
in the sixties or so.
O Lord my God
send down some rain,
though not a flood
just enough to ease my pain.
Lord let me know
via the rainbow
if you hear my prayer
'cause, I know you care.
Amen.

By Dennis Andrew Massei
07-08-2021

115.
God the Only One

Somewhat cool this afternoon
thank you, Lord,
for the rain,
it was you I assume
that eased my pain.
Thank you, Lord,
for looking after me
you're always there
and I can see
the wisdom in your care.
A long time ago
on my way to the store,
a man grabbed ten dollars
out of my hand,
I was ten years old or so
dumbfounded and betrayed
and couldn't understand.
I wasn't harmed in any way
'cause you protected me that day,
just like you always do
Lord I'll always be grateful to you.
I've always said the Lord watches over me,

I could state many occasions this has been done
the list is too long so I'll let it be,
I know it was God he's the only one.

By Dennis Andrew Massei
07-09-2021

116.
Little Brown Jug

A little brown jug
I used to have,
fell on the rug
and broke, it made me mad.
Little brown jug,
with red roses
my favorite kind,
gotta find something else
it's the only thing on my mind.
Found a new jug for my roses
this one's kelly green,
my favorite color
it goes with the scene.
Little green jug
this plastic one I can take,
if it falls on the rug
I doubt it'll break.
Little green jug
holding my roses
what a beautiful scent,

I love the smell of roses
best money I ever spent.

By Dennis Andrew Massei
07-10-2021

155

117.
Lord Take Me, I'm Yours

I wanna go to heaven someday,
Lord, take me, I'm yours
and lead the way,
I'll never again go astray
as I kneel at the cross and pray.
Lord, take me, I'm yours
come into my heart,
I've followed you from my life's start
guide me through my life
and death when I part.
Lord, take me, I'm yours
come into my soul,
as I set my heavenly goal.
Lord, take me, I'm yours
set me free and make me pure,
Lord, take me, I'm yours
I wanna be ready,
when I step on heaven's shore.

By Dennis Andrew Massei
7-10-2021

118.
My Life Depends on You

If the light that I saw

is what made Jesus call

then I'm glad I saw the light.

There's something about God's word that's trusting and true

and if I keep believing,

I'll never be blue.

I'm trying with all my might

to keep on living right,

if I falter Lord tell me what to do

my life depends on you.

Lord give me the strength to be strong

and keep me from doing wrong. God be my power in all that I do

and my faith will always be true.

By Dennis Andrew Massei
07-11-2021

119.
My Faith is Strong and Forever True

I've served the Lord in many ways
in all my living days,
Lord, tell me what else I can do,
my faith is strong and forever true.
God, if it be your will
I'll continue,
It's because of my beliefs
I do these things for you.
Lord, if there's anything I missed
or if I did it wrong, please dismiss.
I've served the Lord my whole life through,
my faith is strong and forever true.
I'll never regret when you entered my heart,
I'm grateful, my life you've been a part.
I ask again what else can I do?
My faith is strong and forever true.
Lord, tell me again
how you dismissed my sin,
I'll always be grateful to you
my faith is strong and forever true.

I wanna hear it again Lord so tell me, how you entered my
soul and made me free,
my heart is pure again too,
my faith is strong and forever true.

By Dennis Andrew Massei
07-13-2021

120.
I'd Do it All over Again

If I had my life to do over
I'd do it, all over again,
grade school, I'd do better than I did,
I had, too much fun being a kid.
In high school, I'd exceed expectation,
and have more honor, at graduation.
I'd go to college to be, what I wanted to be,
but when I look in a mirror,
a shipper is who I see.
I'm proud of the job I do today
and when I can, I go to church and pray,
if I had my life to do over
I'd do it, all over again,
I'd be a chef and a caterer
and live a better life than I planned back then.
If I had my life to do over
I'd do it all over again,
I'd go to college to learn creative writing,
and write better poems than I did back then.

By Dennis Andrew Massei
07-13-2021

121.
Lord I Will Go

Lord I will go
I wanna help
tell me what to do
I can do it by myself.
I can feed the hungry
I can talk the depressed out of dying,
whatever the case may be
please know I'm trying.
Lord I will go
I wanna see
let me know
if my work is effective,
it's important to me.
Lord I will go
on this trip alone
and if there's trouble
I'll conquer it on my own.
Lord I wanna go
no, I don't need any help

I will let you know
if I can't do it by myself.

By Dennis Andrew Massei
07-14-2021

162

122.
Gold Star Praise

If I had a gold star
for every good deed I did
going back years afar
to when I was a kid.
I'd need a giant jar
to keep them all in
for every gold star
God forgave a sin.
To take a gold star
is like the Lord giving me pay
good deeds enough will lead me far,
when I'm ready for heaven someday.
I don't need a gold star
or recognition and fame
I'd shout to heaven afar
to praise his holy name.

07-14-2021

123.
History of the Manger

This manger belonged to Jesus, he died to save all of us.
From the sins we commit every day, and so we all must
kneel and pray.
Jesus lived a long, long time ago,
and we all came to know.
As the son of God,
he gave us all the nod.
In our fight against sin,
thanks to Jesus we can all win.
So, follow our savior
follow him all the way,
he'll judge our behavior
when he returns someday.
Your life is owned
by a savior well known,
and Jesus will come
to lead you home.

07-17-2021

124.

Emptiness

Always and forever
I will love my mother,
I dread the day when we must part
it'll, leave a hole in my heart.
She's more than a mom to me
a friend is who I see
without her here would leave a hole,
in my soul.
She's my teacher too
in all that I do,
great Moms are hard to find
especially one, so caring and kind.
I love you Mother dear
if you weren't here,
I'll feel left behind
with a hole in my mind.
If life treats me unfair
Mother you're always there,

I'll tell you something very true,
my life would be empty, without you.

By Dennis Andrew Massei
07-20-2021

125.
Don't Call Me Lonesome

Don't call me lonesome
'cause I'm feeling blue
I believe in God
his son is my friend that's true.
Don't call me lonesome
I do what I do
as long as Jesus is my friend
I'll never be blue.
Don't call me lonesome
I am not alone
Jesus will lead me
now and when I'm gone.
Don't call me lonesome
this life I don't own
since I follow Jesus
my fate became known.

By Dennis Andrew Massei
07-23-2021

126.
Storms

Storms through the night
dear Lord I pray,
my family and friends
are safe as we awake this day.
May the damage be light
as we all survive the night.
Lord whatever you do
put the burden on those who abandoned you,
for I, my family and friends have not, and are thankful for
all we got.
Show us your mercy
give us some peace,
I pray in Jesus' name
these storms will cease.
Amen.

By Dennis Andrew Massei
07-30-2021

127.
God is Watching

I see God peeking down at me today,
he caught me kneeling getting ready to pray.
Doesn't matter he saw me
as long as I can see,
he knows what I go through
and that my faith is true.
I hope God keeps watching me
and knowing what I'm gonna say,
as long as he keeps caring
I'll never go astray.
When God takes my hand
in heaven someday I'll roam,
that faraway land
where God will lead me home.

By Dennis Andrew Massei
07-31-2021

128.

Thank God for Moms Like You

Your tender touch, the gleam in your eyes,

sets off a glow brighter than sunny skies.

The advice you give, with the good deeds you do, thank God

for Moms like you.

Your gleaming smile, the love in your heart, you convey to

us, that's where it all starts.

The touch of your hand paints a picture so true,

why we all thank God for Moms like you.

Your caring thoughts and the little things you say, your

presence we hold so dear day after day. Your love to us and

our love's so true, thank God for Moms like you.

The love we feel is so strong, Mom, you're very seldom

wrong.

If I die before this world is through,

I, at least, thanked God for Moms like you.

By Dennis Andrew Massei
05-07-1994

129.

Thank God for Dads Like You

For teaching me to ride a bike without training wheels, and how to throw a baseball and hit it too, for talking to me 'bout that girl I was in love with head over heels, thank God for Dads like you.

For cheering me up when I felt sad, giving me the benefit of your experience too, the firm way you handled me when I was simply bad,

thank God for Dads like you. For sharing with me the wisdom of your years, for being there for me too, if only to take away my fears, thank God for Dads like you.

Now I bring this poem to an end, I've nothing left to say or do,

you were not only my dad but a very dear friend, thank God for Dads like you.

By Dennis Andrew Massei
06-16-2013

130.

A Portrait of My Dad

He was a warm-hearted man thinking of others all the time,
always giving whatever he can
even if only a dime.
Nice guys it seems have little to give,
oh Lord how much class he had, the little things he had, he
knew how to live, that's a portrait of my dad.
He was a soft-spoken man, almost in a whisper most of the
time, he was a baseball fan, and he went to church when the
bells chimed. Although he hadn't much wealth,
oh Lord how much class he had, unfortunately he didn't
know his poor health, just another portrait of my dad.

By Dennis Andrew Massei
04-27-1992

131.
Born to the Blues

My story begins a long time ago, way back when I was born
to the blues, here I am still lonesome and so, I guess at love
I'm always gonna lose.
My story's the same as each year passes by,
why I'm so lonesome there aren't any clues,
sometimes I could lay down my head and die,
I keep wishing I wasn't born to the blues.
Lord if you could find a mate for me, you know I've been
paying my dues, being lonesome instead of happy,
I guess I was born to the blues.
The day I die my story will end,
'cause there was no one my lonesome heart to mend,
my story's still the same old bad news,
on my stone it'll say born to the blues.

By Dennis Andrew Massei

132.
My Frisky

I remember when I six years old, in nineteen sixties eight. My dad brought home a stray dog, don't go near him yet I was told, he's full of fleas and ticks you'll just have to wait. After Mom and her friend cleaned him up good, I played with him in the backyard 'cause I knew I could. Scratching and wheezing I called him Frisky, he took an instant like to me.

He'd follow me everywhere I'd go, wherever I was that's where he'd be. I love my Frisky so, my pug my friend just Frisky and me.

It didn't take him long at all, to fetch and return a rubber ball. If it weren't for school, I'd play with him all day. It would've been real cool, my Frisky and me at play.

Somebody opened the front door one day, my Frisky quickly ran astray. Into the street he went and hit by a car, in my heart I can still feel the scar.

We drove my Frisky to the animal doctor, my dad and me, he's at peace now the doctor said just let him be. My tears fell like rain that day, when I learned my Frisky passed away, I wished back then we didn't have to part, my friend my Frisky is forever in my heart.

07-19-2018

133.
Wherever Jesus Goes

I want to be;
Where Jesus goes.
Oh, woe with the world;
God only knows.
Listen to me;
Lord I've got something to say.
I'll always be with you;
Following all the way.
I'm praying for the world;
To have a better way of life.
To have world peace;
Without pain troubles or strife.
I want to know;
What Jesus knows.
I'll follow him;
Wherever he goes.

Another year has passed,
this makes thirty-two.
It won't be the last,
because I'll always miss you.
You were so caring and kind,

and you're always on my mind.
I miss you more each day,
I can still hear you pray.
You're in my heart that keeps you near,
never a man missed his dad more.
I wish you were still here,
and our lives go on as before.
I got tears in my eyes,
oh, what'll I do.
Happy birthday Dad,
In memory of you.

By Dennis Andrew Massei
Missing his dad.

Anthony P. Massei Jr.
January 30, 1936–October 17, 1991

134.
The Golden Terrace of Heaven

On the golden terrace of heaven
that's where I'm destined to be,
precious Jesus is my savior
I know him and he knows me.

I went to Sunday school
when I was a kid,
I thought it was pretty cool
the wonderful things Jesus did.

I learned that Jesus is God's son
and all things are possible
through Jesus thy will be done.

I believe in the holy Bible
I received mine when I was eleven,
after I pass on its where I'll be
on the golden terrace of heaven.

07-02-2022

135.
Jesus, Will You Come Today?

Jesus come Jesus come
will you come right away?
Lord the world is troubled
and I can't help but to pray.
Lord, I love my country
the good old USA,
Jesus come,
will you come today.
Jesus come Jesus come
to lend your mighty hand,
Jesus come Jesus come
come now and heal our land.
Jesus come Jesus come
will you come right away?
Lord the world is troubled
and I can't help but to pray.
Lord, I love all countries
besides the USA,
Jesus come,
bring peace to Ukraine
will you come today?
Jesus come Jesus come

to lend your mighty hand,
Jesus come Jesus come
come now and heal our land.
Jesus come Jesus come
will you come right away?
Lord, the world is troubled
and I can't help but to pray.
Lord, I love all countries
besides the USA,
Jesus, will you come today?
God bless
Taiwan, South Korea and the rest,
may all the world be forever blessed.
Jesus come Jesus come
to lend your mighty hand,
Jesus come Jesus come
come now and heal our land.

07-01-2022

136.
Drive Safe

Precious Lord guide me;
To always drive safe.
Beyond the traffic let me see;
Red light as I stop
for safety is worth the wait.
Precious Lord, control my composure;
if other drivers are reckless and unsafe.
May them find their peace;
As I come to a stop I'd rather wait.
Precious Lord, to you I pray;
Please keep me out of harm's way.
Red lights and stop signs
are meant to keep us safe;
I'd rather follow slowly
for safety is worth the wait.
Precious Lord guide me
to always drive safe.

08-30-2022

137.

Lord If You See Me Like This

I'll drink till I'm falling down
and can't see all around;
Lord if you see me like this
grant my fondest wish.
I'm constantly walking around;
With my head looking down.
Lord if you see the way I roam;
Please, lead me home.
I won't touch the hard stuff;
Beer is enough.
I'll drink till I'm unable to roam;
and pray the Lord leads me home.
Keep bringing me a beer;
Till I'm unable to think.
Lord, I see you are near;
I'm ready! This is my final drink.

09-01-2022
Inspired by a long-gone blues man.

138.

Precious Lord

Precious Lord, bless my family, friends and me;
Take our hearts make them pure,
take our souls and set us free.
Precious Lord we have sinned and done you wrong, now in
our faith we are strong.
It's great to be forgiven and start life anew;
Precious Lord we vow to worship only you.
Precious Lord the world I will tell;
In our sickness you healed us well.
Our world once seemed dark;
Now it's looking bright.
We once walked in sin;
Now precious Lord, we see the light.
Precious Lord, bless my family, friends and me;
Take our hearts make them pure,
take our souls and set us free.

08-25-2022

139.
Denny's Nighttime Prayer

Now I lay me down to sleep
praying God wakes me up tomorrow,
with nothing to make me weep
especially pain and sorrow.
Here I go into dream land
precious Lord my heart to keep,
and help me understand
the problems I reap.
When my dreams end
and I'm awake,
precious Lord my trusted friend
guide me in the decisions I make.
Lord if you take me tonight
bless my family and friends with your love,
and explain to them why you need me
up there in heaven above, Amen.

03-05-2022

140.

Lord, I Cater to You

I am here now
Lord what can I do?
Here I am Lord
I cater to you.
All my love Lord
so loyal and true,
will be the same Lord
my whole life through.
I praise your name Lord
wherever I am,
I will do more Lord
whenever I can.
I am here now
Lord I'm glad I came,
Here I am Lord
to praise your holy name.
I am here now
is there more I can do?
Here I am Lord
I cater to you.
I am here now
ready to do good deeds,

Here I am Lord
you've catered to my needs.
Now it's my turn
to do something for you,
Here I am Lord
I cater to you.

0919-2021

141.
On the Side of Caution

I'm on the side of caution
when I tell you I've been saved,
I'll do right by the Lord
for my sins he forgave.
I'm on the side of caution
you should do the same,
be on the side of caution
and praise his holy name.
On the side of caution
I'll go to church and pray,
I'm taking precautions
by doing good deeds each day.
I'm on the side of caution
by letting Jesus lead the way,
for when I get heaven
I know, I'll be there to stay.

11-2-2021

142.

Jesus Has a Way to Punish Me

When I was a lad
playing happily
I loved Mom and Dad
who treated me tenderly.
Except when I was bad
it sure made me sad
when they punished me.
Now a God-fearing man
I came to be known
I devised a plan,
to be good
now that I'm grown.
Sometimes I go astray
drinking with friends
I've longed to see.
Now it's Jesus
with a subtle way
to punish me.
He'll allow me a beer or two maybe more than a few.
Then make me sick
the next day
causing me to lose a day's pay.

Jesus has a way,
a very subtle way
to punish me.
He'll allow me a small win
in the lottery,
then give extra bills
I didn't see.
Dear Lord how I do pray
I will always welcome
your subtle way,
Jesus has a way
to punish me.
Now I'll tow line
till the day I'm gone,
good will is mine
and I'd love to pass it on.
For the love of Jesus
no more a sinner I'll be
Jesus has a way,
to punish me.

02-19-2022

143.

I'm the Eyes of the Lord

When the Lord
calls me,
I tell him
everything I see.
In the eyes
of the Lord,
I'm a trustee.
The evil I see
that's all around,
it is my job
to face the devil down.
I'm the eyes of the Lord
judge in his highest court,
watchdog of the Earth
an evil police of sorts.
I'm the ears of the Lord
and I can hear it all,
I will praise his holy name
the day all evil shall fall.
Power in my nose
and I can sense,
the evil miles away

making good people tense.
Blessed are the peacemakers
and I identify as one,
I vow to never quit
until my life is done.

01-13-2022

Jesus Comes and Goes With Me

Jesus comes and goes
With me,
And the sins he forgave
That made me free.
Jesus comes and goes
And I bet he's the only one who knows,
'bout the problems and strife,
Plaguing me my whole life.
I learned early on
He'll love me long after I'm gone,
His love fits to a tee
Jesus comes and goes with me
Through his promise of eternal life
They'll be no more pain or strife,
When I go to dwell with he
Jesus comes and goes, with me.

The Sweetest Thing

The sweetest thing;
I ever saw.

A little boy;

And his dog.

Romping around;

The front yard.

A playful growl

And a giggling sound.

The sweetest thing;

I'll ever know.

A new born baby;

Smiling so.

Purity and Innocence;

In that toothless grin.

A beautiful child;

Without a sin.

The sweetest thing.

I'll ever see.

Beautiful flowers;

Blooming in the spring.

Young lovers;

In a sweet embrace.

A wonderful smile;

Upon their face.

The sweetest thing;.

When all conflicts cease.

It's a beautiful world;

When we have peace.

By Dennis Andrew Massei

06-25-2023